Spots

and Other Lumps and Bumps

Elspeth Graham

OXFORD

UNIVERSITY PRESS

OXFORD
UNIVERSITY PRESS

Great Clarendon Street, Oxford OX2 6DP

Oxford University Press is a department of the University of Oxford.
It furthers the University's objective of excellence in research, scholarship,
and education by publishing worldwide in

Oxford New York

Athens Auckland Bangkok Bogotá Buenos Aires Calcutta
Cape Town Chennai Dar es Salaam Delhi Florence Hong Kong Istanbul
Karachi Kuala Lumpur Madrid Melbourne Mexico City Mumbai
Nairobi Paris São Paulo Shanghai Singapore Taipei Tokyo Toronto Warsaw

with associated companies in Berlin Ibadan

Oxford is a registered trade mark of Oxford University Press
in the UK and in certain other countries

Published in the United Kingdom
by Oxford University Press

British Library Cataloguing in Publication Data

Data available

ISBN 0 19 917369 9

Available in packs
The Human Body   Pack of Four (one of each book)   ISBN 0 19 917372 9
The Human Body   Class Pack (six of each book)   ISBN 0 19 917373 7

Printed in Hong Kong

Acknowledgements

The Publisher would like to thank the following for permission
to reproduce photographs:

p 4 The Image Bank/Tracy Frankel, p 5 Science Photo Library/Dr P Marazzi (left),
SPL/A Syred (right), pp 7, 9 SPL, p 12 Corbis UK (top), Corel (bottom), pp 15,
16 SPL, p 17 SPL/C Nuridsay & M Perennou (top), SPL/S Camazine (bottom),
Oxford Scientific Films (right), p 18 SPL, p 19 SPL/Satun Stills (top), SPL (all),
p 20 Corbis UK, p 21 SPL/B Wolff, p 22 Corbis UK (top), Mary Evans Picture
Library (centre and left).

Front cover: SPL & John Holder
Back cover: Graham Round

Illustrations by Julian & Janet Baker, John Holder, Graham Round,
Darryl Warner

Contents

Introduction   4

Under your skin   5

Blackheads, pimples, and acne   6

Lumps   8

Bumps   10

Patterns and patches   12

Allergies   14

Bites and stings   16

Spots that are catching   18

Bubonic plague   22

Conclusion   23

Glossary   24

Index   24

Introduction

Skin covers your body from head to toe.
It is waterproof, stretchy and helps to protect
your body from injury or **infection**.

Sometimes skin gets spotty. There are
lots of different kinds of spots, lumps,
bumps, and swellings. Most spots,
lumps and bumps are normal:
everyone has a few. Other spots are
signs of disease, such as measles or
chicken pox. There are spots which
have been caused by bites or stings
from insects such as fleas, mosquitoes,
or wasps. Some people have **sensitive**
skin and come out in spots if they
touch certain things.

Under your skin

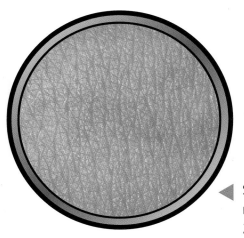

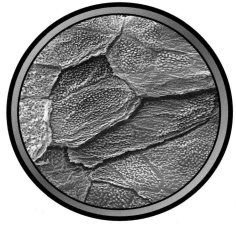

◀ Skin seen under a **microscope**, magnified 265 times (left) and 1330 times (right). ▼

outer layer of skin

pore

hair

oil gland

follicle

sweat gland

blood vessel

layer of fat

◀ A cross-section through a layer of skin. Hair grows from tiny pits in the skin called follicles. There are also follicles where there is no hair. Each follicle has a **gland** which makes oil to keep the skin soft, supple and waterproof.

FACT BOX

Skin helps to control our body temperature. It cools the body down with sweat and it grows hair to keep us warm.

Blackheads, pimples, and acne

Blackheads

Sometimes a follicle gets blocked up with a thick plug of oil and dead skin **cells**. Light and air turn the plug a dark colour. This is called a blackhead.

Never pick or squeeze a blackhead. That will make it easier for **germs** to enter and make the spot worse.

Pimples

If oil builds up under a blackhead, the spot becomes bigger. Germs may multiply in the trapped oil. This makes the surrounding skin red and sore. The blackhead becomes a raised, reddened sore spot, or pimple.

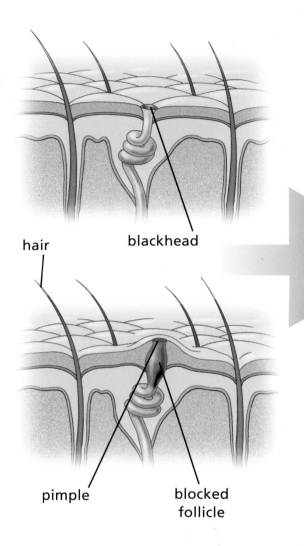

hair

blackhead

pimple

blocked follicle

FACT **BOX**

The number of germs living on your skin is about the same as the number of people living in the world!

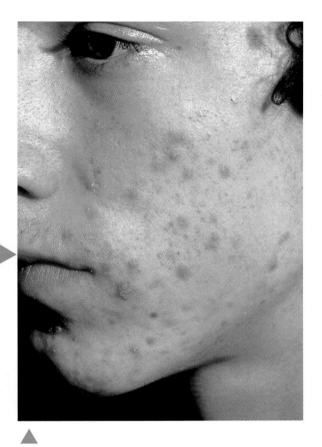

▲ A teenager with acne.

FACT BOX

When the mummy of Ramesses II was examined, scientists found that he had had terrible blackheads.

Acne

Acne is the pimples and blackheads that almost all teenagers get at some time. The name "acne" comes from a Greek word meaning "face eruption". People with acne can get creams and medicines from a chemist or doctor to help clear it up.

Lumps

Warts

Warts are lumps on the skin caused by a **virus**. The virus makes the skin's cells multiply quickly to form firm, usually round, lumps. Warts are mostly harmless and usually disappear after a year or so. However, because they are **contagious**, it's a good idea to treat them. A chemist or doctor will be able to give advice on curing them.

Folklore cures for warts

There are lots of strange cures for warts, such as rubbing the wart with a snail, or "selling" the wart to someone. One very old cure for a wart was to lay half a mouse on it for half-an-hour and then bury the mouse in the ground. As the mouse rotted away, the wart was supposed to disappear too.

Ingrowing warts

Verrucas are a kind of wart that grows on the soles of the feet. A verruca grows into the foot, not out of it. The pressure of body weight forces them to grow inwards.

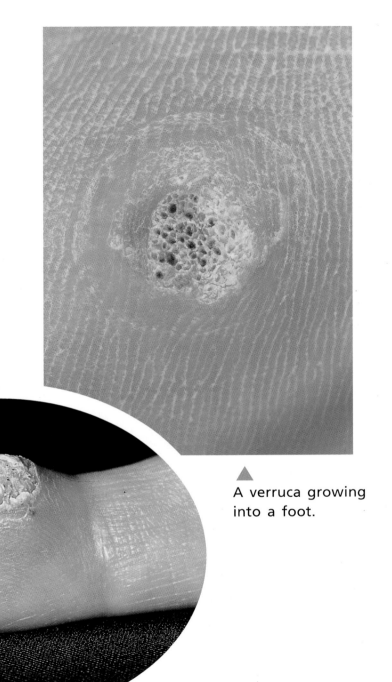

▲ A verruca growing into a foot.

▲ A wart growing out of a finger.

Bumps

Goosebumps

Trapping heat

When we are cold, our skin gets covered in goosebumps (or goosepimples). This is because our skin tries to stop heat escaping by pulling the hairs upright. This traps a layer of warm air next to the body.

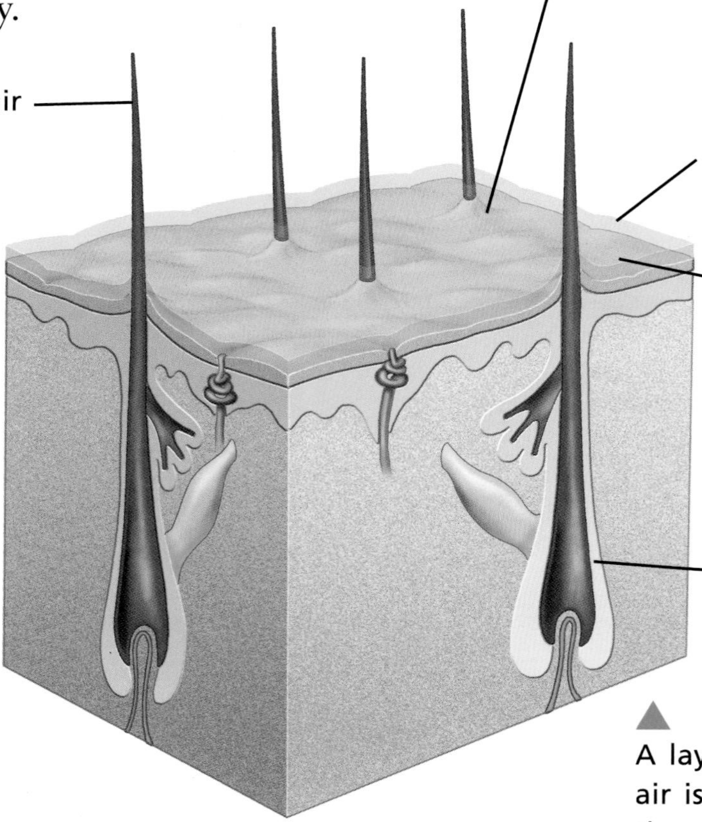

goosebump

hair

layer of warm air

skin

hair follicle

A layer of warm air is trapped by the upright hairs.

Some people call skin that is covered in goosebumps "chicken skin". Next time you get goosebumps, look at the skin on your arms. Does it look like the skin of a plucked chicken?

Self-defence

We also get goosebumps when we are scared. The best way to understand why this happens is to watch a cat when it is scared by the approach of a dog. The fur all over the cat sticks out. This makes the cat look much bigger and fiercer, and will often make a dog think again before attacking.

Not very many people are hairy enough for this to work very well! However, fright can raise the hairs on the back of our necks.

Patterns and patches

Skin colour

Skin gets its colour from melanin. Melanin protects us from damage by the sun. In strong sunlight, skin makes more melanin. People with dark-coloured skins have more melanin naturally.

Freckles

A freckle is a tiny area of the skin with extra melanin in it. Freckles are always flat and can be scattered in patterns across the body. Freckles darken in summer and fade in winter.

Moles

Like freckles, moles also contain extra melanin. Moles are darker than freckles and are usually raised into small bumps. People have fewer moles than freckles. Moles on the face are sometimes called "beauty spots". If you have a mole and it suddenly begins to grow, change colour, or bleed, then you should go to a doctor.

Patches

During the 17th and 18th centuries, it was fashionable for men and women to wear small black patches or beauty spots.

Patches were cut out of black silk or velvet and stuck onto the skin. Sun, moon, and star shapes were popular. Some shapes were much more complicated, for example tiny flowers or even sailing ships. In fact, these beauty spots usually covered up some ugly scar or blemish.

Allergies

Rashes

When skin comes up in small red spots, it is known as a rash. Some people get rashes if they touch certain things, for example jewellery, metal watch straps, or washing powders.

Allergic reactions

An allergy is when the body reacts badly to something which is normally harmless. Allergies can cause a runny nose, sore eyes, a rash on the skin, or difficulty in breathing.

This girl has been eating strawberries and her skin has come up in itchy red lumps called hives.

▼

FACT BOX

Some people are allergic to certain foods like cows' milk, wheat, cheese, peanuts, strawberries, or shellfish. Some people are allergic to food additives. Some people are allergic to medicines, for example **penicillin**.

Tests can be done to find out what is causing an allergic reaction. Tiny amounts of things which may be the cause are pricked into the skin. If a spot or blister comes up, it shows which one is the cause of the allergy.

When you touch a nettle, each prickle releases a small amount of weak poison. Your skin then becomes covered in a rash that stings and itches.

Nettles are covered in fine prickles.

A rash caused by nettles.

Bites and stings

There are many different insects that bite or sting. Most bites and stings are harmless. Others can be painful or even dangerous.

Insects that bite

When some insects (such as mosquitoes, fleas, lice, or ticks) bite people, itchy bumps form on the skin. This is because when they bite they also inject some **saliva**. This causes an allergic reaction. Although the bumps may be very itchy, they disappear quickly.

A head louse, magnified 54 times, clinging to a human hair.

FACT BOX

Malaria

A bite from the anopheles mosquito can be dangerous! Only the female anopheles mosquito bites people. When she does, she injects the malaria **germ** from earlier victims. She passes the disease "malaria" on from person to person.

Malaria is a deadly disease that exists in tropical countries. The main signs of malaria are fever, shivering, and becoming soaked in sweat. Millions of people die each year from malaria.

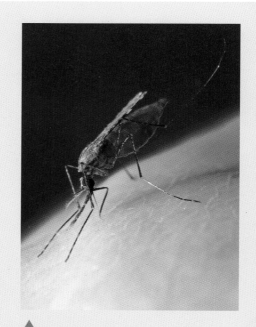

Malaria mosquito biting human skin.

Insects that sting

Bees, wasps, and hornets are all insects that sting. Their stings can be painful, but are usually only dangerous for people who are allergic to the poison. The swelling and pain should disappear in a few hours.

A bee sting.

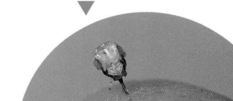

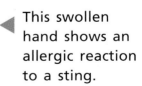

This swollen hand shows an allergic reaction to a sting.

Spots that are catching

Measles and chickenpox are infectious diseases. This means they can be passed from one person to another.

Measles

Measles usually affects children under six. The first sign of measles is tiny white spots found inside the cheek. Then millions of tiny dark red spots form on the skin. The spots join up to form blotches. Measles is a serious disease. An **injection** can often stop it being caught.

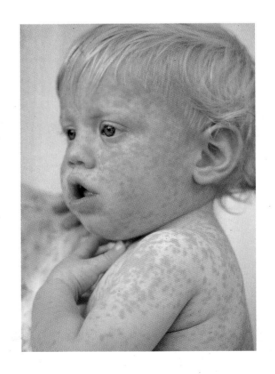

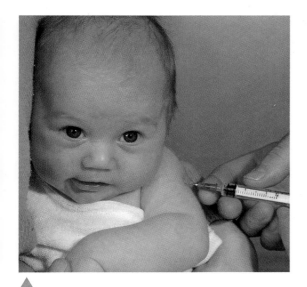

Most babies are given an injection to protect them from measles.

German measles

German measles, or rubella, usually affects older children and teenagers. A rash of tiny pink spots appears. The spots may be so close together that they look like a solid mass of pink. German measles is usually a mild disease. It is serious when a pregnant woman catches it because the disease can badly damage her baby.

Chickenpox

Chickenpox usually affects children under ten. They get itchy red spots all over the body, even in the mouth. The spots turn into blisters which then dry out and form scabs. If you have chickenpox you should try not to scratch the spots. If the spots get infected you should see a doctor.

An itchy rash of chickenpox spots covers this child's body.

Chickenpox blisters

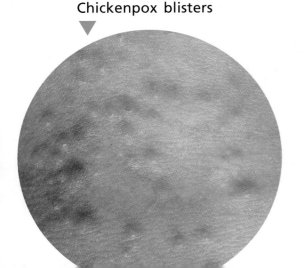

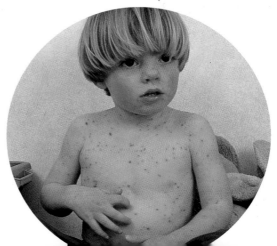

Smallpox and cowpox

Smallpox was a deadly disease.
It was caught by breathing in a **virus**.
The signs of the disease were high
fever, sores, and pus-filled spots.
There was a rash all over the body,
which was worst on the face. In the
past, many people died of smallpox
and others were left scarred and
often blind.

◄ This boy, who
caught smallpox in
1973, is covered
with smallpox scars.

Jenner and vaccination

Edward Jenner (1749–1823) was a doctor. He heard that milkmaids who had caught a mild disease called cowpox did not later catch smallpox. After years of careful study, he gave an eight-year-old boy a dose of cowpox and, when the boy got better, he dosed him with smallpox. The boy did not become ill. Jenner called this method of protection against smallpox **vaccination**. The Latin word for cow is "vacca".

Edward Jenner giving eight-year-old James Phipps the first vaccination against smallpox in 1796.

▼

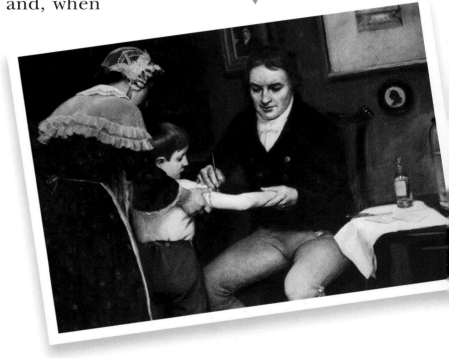

1967	1978	1980
• The World Health Organization begins a campaign to rid the world of smallpox. • About 10–15 million cases of smallpox occur each year. Of these cases, at least 2 million people die.	• One person develops smallpox but survives.	• The World Health Organization says that it now believes that smallpox has been wiped out.

Source: WHO

Bubonic plague

In Europe during the Middle Ages, millions of people died from the **plague**. There are few cases of the plague nowadays. Catching the plague used to mean certain death. Now the chances of survival are 95 per cent or better.

Bubonic plague is carried by rat fleas. One symptom of the plague is buboes. Buboes are swellings that first appear in the armpits, groin or on the neck. They can grow as big as chicken eggs.

'Ring a ring of roses'

Ring a ring of roses,
A pocketful of posies,
Atishoo, atishoo,
We all fall down.

◀ This rhyme is thought to be about the plague. Buboes looked like "rings of roses"; posies of flowers were carried for protection against the disease; sneezing was a sign that someone had caught the plague.

Conclusion

People have always had spots, lumps, and bumps on their skin. Some spots are normal and may be thought of as beautiful. Other spots can be a sign of a problem.

Spots and pimples are caused by too much oil in the skin. Freckles and moles are caused by extra melanin. Rashes, blotches and swellings are signs of an allergy or disease. Itchy lumps can be the result of insect bites.

In an effort to clear up their skin, people have tried some strange cures in the past. However, some cures have helped to get rid of diseases.

Glossary

acne Reddened, sore pimples on the face, neck, shoulders, and upper chest.

cell The tiniest part of a living thing. A body is made up of millions of cells.

contagious Can be passed on by touching someone or something already infected.

eradicate To get rid of something.

germ A tiny living thing which can cause illness.

gland A part of the body that makes something which is useful to the body.

infection When germs get into the body.

injection Putting medicine into the body with a hollow needle.

microscope An instrument that makes it possible to see very tiny things, by making them seem much bigger.

penicillin A common medicine.

plague A dangerous illness that spreads very quickly.

saliva A liquid made in the mouth to help break down food.

sensitive Reacts very easily or strongly.

vaccination A weak dose of a disease given so that the body learns to fight it.

virus A very tiny germ that can cause a disease by changing the way cells work.

Index

acne 7
allergies 14–15, 17
beauty spots 12–13
bites 16
blackhead 6, 7
bubonic plague 22
chickenpox 19
cowpox 21
fleas 16, 22
freckles 12
German measles 19
germs 6, 16
goosebumps 10–11
hives 14
Jenner 20–21
measles 18
moles 12
mosquitoes 16
oil 5-6
pimple 6
rashes 14-15, 19
saliva 16
scabs 19
scars 13, 20
smallpox 20–21
stings 17
swellings 17, 22
vaccination 21
virus 8
warts 8–9

Lifesavers

DISCOVERIES IN MEDICINE

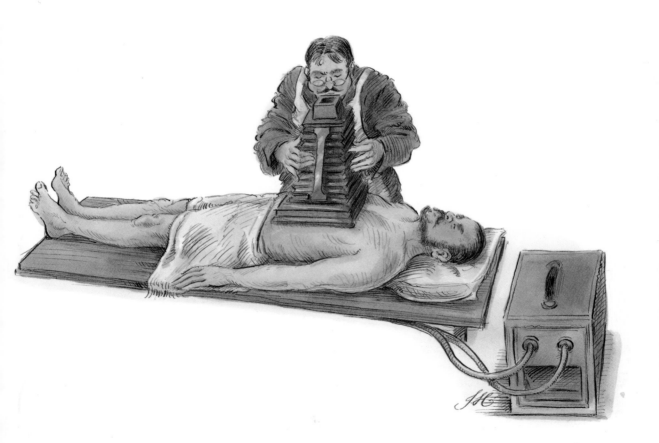

Jacqueline Dineen

OXFORD
UNIVERSITY PRESS

OXFORD
UNIVERSITY PRESS

Great Clarendon Street, Oxford OX2 6DP

Oxford University Press is a department of the University of Oxford.
It furthers the University's objective of excellence in research, scholarship,
and education by publishing worldwide in

Oxford New York

Auckland Bangkok Buenos Aires Cape Town Chennai
Dar es Salaam Delhi Hong Kong Istanbul Karachi Kolkata
Kuala Lumpur Madrid Melbourne Mexico City Mumbai
Nairobi São Paulo Shanghai Taipei Tokyo Toronto

Oxford is a registered trade mark of Oxford University Press
in the UK and in certain other countries

Published in the United Kingdom
by Oxford University Press

Text © Jacqueline Dineen 2001
The moral rights of the author have been asserted

Database right Oxford University Press (maker)

First published 2001
10 9 8 7 6 5 4 3

British Library Cataloguing in Publication Data

Data available

ISBN 0 19 917450 4

Also available in packs

Explorers and Discoveries Inspection Pack (one of each book) ISBN 0 19 917452 0
Explorers and Discoveries Class Pack (six of each book) ISBN 0 19 917453 9

Acknowledgements

The Publisher would like to thank the following for permission to reproduce photographs:

Bridgeman Art Library/ Bibliotheque Royal de Belgique, Brussels, Belgium: p 13 (right); Bridgeman Art
Library/Musee des Beaux-Arts, Marseilles,France/Giraudon: p 15 (top); Bridgeman Art Library/Santa
Maria of Egara in Terrasssa, Barcelona, Spain: p 10: Corbis: pp 6 (bottom), 8 (top), 21 (bottom);
Corbis S.A.Archivo Iconografico: p 11 (bottom); Corbis/Bettmann: pp 11 (top), 13 (left), 15 (bottom),
21 (top), 25 (bottom left & right); Corbis/Duomo: p 28 (top); Corbis/George Lepp: p 12 (top);
Corbis/Kevin Morris: pp 7 (bottom), 24; Corbis/Richard T Nowitz: p 22; Corbis/Science Pictures Ltd: p
19 (top); C M Dixon: p 6 (top); Hulton Getty: pp 14 (left), 20. 23 (top), 27; Illustrated London News:
p 19 (bottom); Oxford University Press: p 29 (bottom); The Royal College of Physicians: p 17; Science
Photo Library: pp 18 (bottom), 25 (top), 26 (both); Alexander Fleming Laboratory Museum, St Mary's
NHS Trust/St James' Church, Paddington: p 23 (bottom); John Walmsley: p 29 (top); The Wellcome
Trust: pp 7 (top), 8 (bottom), 14 (right), 16 (top), 18 (top); World Health Organization: p 28 (bottom).

Front cover: Telegraph colour Library
Back cover: The Wellcome Trust

Illustrated by: Elizabeth Blackler, Matt Buckley, Stefan Chabluk, David Cuzik, John Holder, Richard
Morris, and Thomas Sperling

Designed by Alicia Howard at Tangerine Tiger

Printed in Hong Kong

Contents

Introduction 4

Medicine men and women 6

Hippocrates and Galen 8

Saints and witches 10

Plague! 12

Renaissance observers and thinkers 14

Medicine in the 17th and 18th centuries 16

Edward Jenner pioneers vaccines 18

Louis Pasteur links germs with disease 19

Hospital pioneers 20

Marie Curie explores radioactivity 22

Alexander Fleming and penicillin 23

DNA and the double helix 24

Modern surgery 26

What next? 28

Glossary 30

Books for further reading 31

Index 32

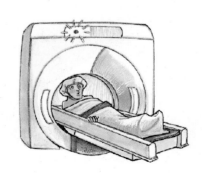

Introduction

From earliest times, men and women have struggled to cure diseases and physical ailments. The first "medicines" were very simple, but as people began to learn more about the human body they discovered and developed new cures and treatments. The pioneering work of these people means that today we live longer, healthier lives than ever before.

Saving lives

The journey of discovery has been a long and exciting one. As people began to understand more about how the human body worked, they were able to study what happens when a person becomes ill. They explored how the body can be weakened by germs and **viruses**, how bones can be broken in different ways, and how organs (such as the heart, lungs, and liver) can become so diseased that they no longer do the job they were designed to do.

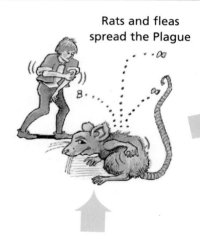

Rats and fleas spread the Plague

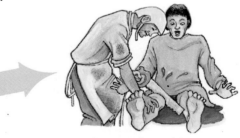

Amputation without painkillers

Herbal medicine

Early brain surgery

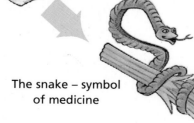

The snake – symbol of medicine

Once people understood more about the body, they were able to invent new equipment and develop new medical techniques. Not only could more diseases and injuries be treated, but patients were cared for in a way that gave them a better chance of recovery.

However, this path of progress was sometimes dangerous. Some early pioneers of new treatments put their own lives at risk, by experimenting on themselves. Others put themselves, unknowingly, in danger, and died early as a consequence. Marie Curie, for example, spent years studying radioactivity, but died from its harmful effects. *See Radioactivity p.22* ➡

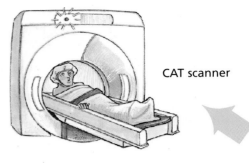

CAT scanner

Other pioneers became disheartened, particularly when their new ideas brought criticism. Andrea Vesalius, for example, burnt all his unpublished works and gave up teaching when his new book on anatomy was ridiculed. *See Vesalius p.15*

Circulation of the blood

Florence Nightingale and nursing

Organ transplants

Leech treatment

Developing the smallpox vaccine

All the men and women featured in this book were lifesavers. It is difficult to calculate exactly how many lives have been saved by their work, but it is millions worldwide. Whenever you take medicine, go to the doctor, have an operation or an injection you are benefiting from the work of these people.

Medicine men and women

Prehistoric peoples did not have medicines as we know them, but they did use plants and herbs with special healing properties. Archaeologists have found pollen grains from healing plants in ancient burial grounds, some of which are 50,000 years old.

Brain surgery with flint

A more drastic form of healing was **trepanning**, an early form of brain surgery. People in Stone Age times believed that headaches were caused by evil spirits in the brain. Their "cure" was to drill a hole into the skull to let the spirits out. Surprisingly, some people survived this operation.

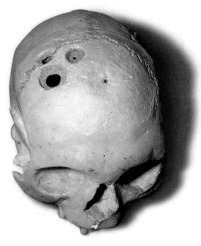

▲ In this ancient man's skull two of the trepanning holes have healed (the edges have become smooth) which means that the man survived two operations. The other hole has not healed, so he must have died after the third operation.

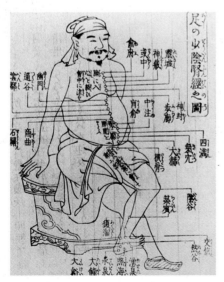

▲ Charts like this one from China, showed doctors the points where acupuncture needles should be inserted.

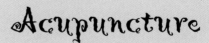

Acupuncture

Some healing methods used in Ancient China are still used today.

The Chinese believed that illness was caused when two forces in the body, *yin* and *yang*, were unbalanced. The balance could be corrected by pushing needles into the body in special places. This treatment is known as **acupuncture**.

▶ The Yin Yang symbol

Early doctors

Healing methods changed once people began to settle down in communities. Documents from about 1500 BC show that medicine in Ancient Egypt involved religion and magic. Medicines were made from plants, minerals, and animal products, such as hippopotamus fat. The doctor chanted a spell as he gave the patient the medicine; the spell was thought to drive evil spirits out of the body.

▶ The first known physician was Imhotep. He was born in 2686 BC and was also chief minister to King Zoser, an early Egyptian pharaoh.

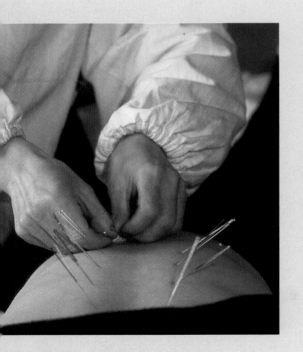

▲ Modern acupuncture treatment

In India, one punishment for disobeying the law was cutting off a person's nose. Indian doctors learnt how create new noses for people, by grafting flaps of skin (taken from the patient) over the stump of the nose and inserting reed tubes to give it shape.

Hippocrates and Galen

Hippocrates (about 460 – 377 BC) lived in Ancient Greece and is known as the "father of modern medicine". Before his time, sick people visited one of the temples dedicated to Asclepius, the Greek god of healing, and the priests treated them with simple remedies.

▼ This stone picture shows a sick woman with the god Asclepius visiting her bedside.

Hippocrates did not rely on a god for healing. He examined patients to try and find the cause of their illness. He studied their **symptoms** and then treated them with suitable medicines. Modern **diagnosis** developed from his methods. Hippocrates founded a school of medicine on the Greek island of Kos. Doctors had to take the Hippocratic Oath, which listed their duties and the ways they should be carried out. Doctors still have to take the Hippocratic Oath today.

◄The symbol that is always linked to Asclepius is a snake, and it is still the symbol of medicine today.

Islamic medicine

After the Roman Empire was conquered in the 5th century AD, there was no more medical teaching in Europe. However, the Arabs studied Greek medical texts and made improvements of their own.

Rhases (AD 865–925), the chief doctor at the hospital in Baghdad (capital city of modern Iraq), was the first medical writer to describe the difference between smallpox and measles.

►The Persian physician Avicenna (AD 980-1037) wrote a book that was used by medical students until the 17th century.

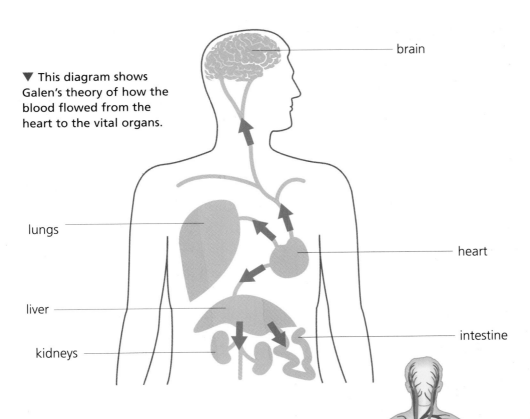

▼ This diagram shows Galen's theory of how the blood flowed from the heart to the vital organs.

brain

lungs

heart

liver

intestine

kidneys

heart

artery

vein

The studies of Galen

Galen (AD 129 – 199) became the most important doctor in Ancient Rome. His first job as a doctor was to treat the wounds of Roman gladiators. By studying the torn limbs and muscles, Galen worked out how the brain controls the muscles of the body.

Galen wanted to make further studies on the human body, but it was forbidden for religious reasons, so he used animals instead. He wrote medical books that doctors were to use for hundreds of years, even though some of his ideas were mistaken. Galen's **theories** were not challenged by other doctors for 1400 years. *See Blood p.16* ➡

▲ This is the modern view of blood circulation. Galen believed that the blood passed from the heart to different parts of the body. He did not realize that it circulates around the body, returning to the heart.

9

Saints and witches

In medieval Europe, the Christian Church taught people that illness was a punishment from God. People prayed to God and made pilgrimages to the shrines of saints in the hope of being cured.

There were a few hospitals, run by nuns or monks, in which sick people were cared for, but there were few real cures. The only medicines were herbal remedies, many of which were prepared by women at home.

Some of these "wise women" were skilled in their work and their herbal mixtures were effective in treating some **ailments**, but many were not. Some people believed that these women had magical powers and were dangerous.

They were accused of being witches and some were even put to death.

Healing plants were made into ointments to rub on wounds, teas to be drunk, or mixtures to be **inhaled**. The witch-hazel plant has been used for many years to soothe wounds, bruising, and burns.

Many doctors believed that disease was caused by the planets. They used a book about the planets, called a *Vademecum*, to diagnose what was wrong with their patients. The book contained charts that showed how to make a **diagnosis** by studying the patient's **urine**. It also had charts showing how to treat ailments by blood-letting.

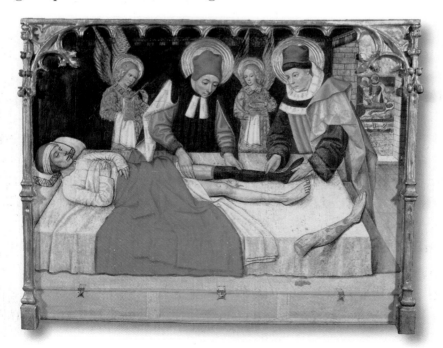

◀ The legendary twins, Cosmos and Damian, were believed to be healing saints. This painting shows them replacing a person's infected leg with the healthy leg of a black man who has just died.

▲ Some doctors believed that blood-letting drained poisons out of the blood. Blood was taken from different parts of the body as a treatment for different illnesses.

▼ By the 14th century, medical schools were teaching more scientific ways of examining urine, using the colour and appearance to help diagnose illnesses.

Early medical schools

At the end of the period known as the Dark Ages (about AD 415 – 825), people became more interested in finding out how the body worked. During the 10th century, doctors looked again at the records of medical knowledge of the Greeks and Romans, and a medical school was founded at Salerno in Italy. Doctors were taught the methods of Hippocrates and Galen, and learned to diagnose illness by looking for **symptoms**.

Plague!

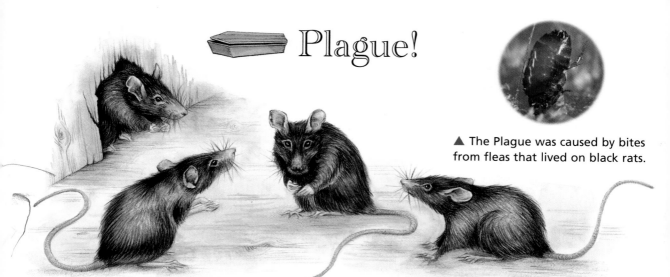

▲ The Plague was caused by bites from fleas that lived on black rats.

The Black Death, also known as the Bubonic Plague, began in China in 1333. It spread to Europe along trade routes from the East.

Hygiene was poor and towns were dirty, so rats thrived. Fleas carrying the Plague quickly spread from rats to other animals and then to people.

People with Bubonic Plague suffered huge swellings, called buboes, in the armpits and the groin. The buboes quickly went black and people died within twelve hours. Rumours about the Plague had spread to Europe before the disease itself arrived in 1346, but doctors did not know how to treat it.

▲ Black rats found their way into goods and onto merchants' ships. People used to believe "No ship rats, no plague!" but this was wrong. Fleas could live for several weeks without going near a rat, and so could travel long distances in ships' cargoes.

Saving their own skin

At the time, no one knew exactly what caused the Plague. Some doctors thought it was caused by bad **vapours** in the air that could enter the body through the skin. They covered themselves with protective clothing from head to foot when treating Plague victims. To avoid touching patients, doctors used a wand to feel the patient's pulse.

The Plague had a **devastating** effect in Europe. About one third of the total population died (more than 25 million people), and whole towns were wiped out.

▲ Doctors wore masks with beaks filled with sweet-smelling herbs and spices. They believed these would purify the air they breathed, and prevent them from catching the Plague.

▼ This painting shows the citizens of Tournai in France carrying coffins of Plague victims to a mass grave.

Leprosy

Leprosy was another disease that was common in Europe at this time. Leprosy affects the skin and nerves, and parts of the body are gradually eaten away. There was no cure in the Middle Ages, so lepers were kept away from other people, usually in hostels run by priests. Leprosy had disappeared from Europe by the 16th century.

Renaissance observers and thinkers

The period known as the "Renaissance" (meaning "rebirth") began in Italy at the end of the 14th century and the changes spread throughout Europe. People studied art, literature, and science from the classical ages of Greece and Rome. Instead of just accepting these old ideas, many people began to question them.

Paracelsus, the Professor of Medicine at the University of Basle in Switzerland, began his lectures by burning books by Avicenna and Galen. *See pages 8 – 9* ←

He said that a doctor should look at his **patients** with his own eyes and not rely on the **theories** of men who had been dead for centuries.

▼ Until the Church allowed people to **dissect** human bodies, models were used to teach students about how the body worked.

Leonardo da Vinci

The Renaissance painter and sculptor Leonardo da Vinci (1452–1519) produced the first detailed drawings of the human **anatomy**. He dissected several bodies and made notes of what he saw.

►Leonardo da Vinci believed that an artist could only show a human body properly if he or she understood how it worked.

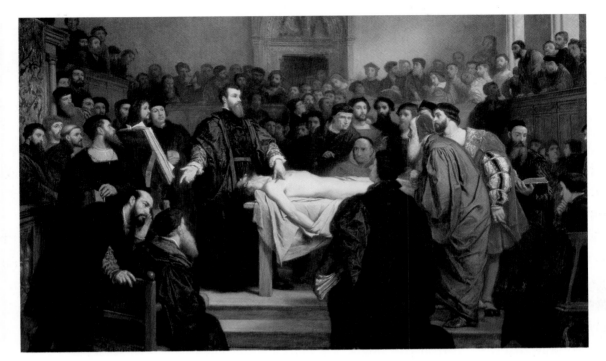

▲ Vesalius eventually pioneered dissections in medical schools, believing it was the only way students could learn in detail about the human body.

Vesalius

Andrea Vesalius (1514 – 64), Professor of Anatomy at Padua University in Italy, believed that doctors could not learn more about the human body without dissecting it. Cutting up dead bodies like this was forbidden by the Church, but Vesalius secretly dissected bodies of criminals stolen from the public gallows.

Vesalius wrote the first great work on human anatomy, *De Humani Corporis Fabrics (On the Structure of the Human Body)*. The book caused arguments because it suggested that some of Galen's theories were wrong.

Ambroise Paré

Ambroise Paré (1541 – 90) was appointed surgeon-general to three French kings. During the war between Italy and France, Paré treated many of the soldiers who lost limbs. Before the Renaissance, most **amputations** killed the patient, but new methods of **surgery** and better understanding of the human body meant that more patients survived. *See p.27* ➡

▲ Paré designed many artificial limbs. Most were made of iron.

Medicine in the 17th and 18th centuries

The new ideas and new methods of studying developed during the Renaissance were continued into the 17th century.

William Harvey

One of the most important discoveries in the history of medicine was made by an English doctor, William Harvey (1578 – 1657). Harvey wanted to find out how the heart worked so he studied live hearts. He discovered that the heart pumps blood around the body, sending it out through the arteries and circulating it back through the veins.

▲ Despite medical progress, many doctors still used worm-like **leeches** which, they believed, sucked out poisons from the blood.

▼ William Harvey used simple experiments to show that the blood flowed in one direction, and that the blood flow to the heart could be stopped by pressing on a vein.

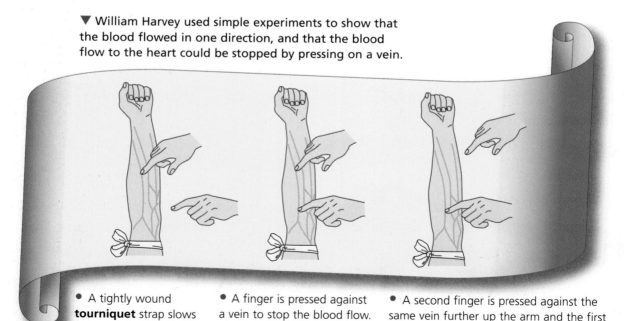

• A tightly wound **tourniquet** strap slows down the blood flow and the **patient's** veins stand out.

• A finger is pressed against a vein to stop the blood flow. A section of the vein empties. Blood does not flow into it from further up the arm.

• A second finger is pressed against the same vein further up the arm and the first finger is released.
The blood flows up from the patient's hand and fills the empty section of the vein.

Anthony van Leeuwenhoek

Anthony van Leeuwenhoek (1632 – 1723) was a Dutch merchant who spent much of his life developing the microscope. Using his microscopes, he was able to study blood cells and microscopic **bacteria**.

Anthony van Leeuwenhoek ground his own lenses and made some which magnified up to 300 times.
See Pasteur p.27 ➡

The Hunter Brothers

Two Scottish brothers, William and John Hunter, pioneered many advances in **anatomy** and **surgery**. John Hunter (1728 – 93), is considered to be the founder of modern surgery. He studied under his elder brother William (1718 – 93), who lectured in anatomy and was a skilled doctor.

▼ William Hunter lecturing about anatomy to his students

Edward Jenner pioneers vaccines

One of the biggest steps taken towards preventing diseases was made by an English doctor, Edward Jenner (1749 – 1823). In the 18th century, smallpox was one of the most dreaded diseases. It is very **contagious** (easily caught by touching someone). In an **epidemic** in 1796, one-fifth of the population of London died from it.

While Jenner was working as a country doctor, he noticed that milkmaids often caught a mild illness, called cowpox, but they never caught the deadly smallpox. This gave him the idea that perhaps the cowpox made them **immune** to smallpox.

▲ This cartoon, published in 1802, played on people's fears about **vaccination**. It shows people turning into cows after being **injected** with the cowpox vaccine.

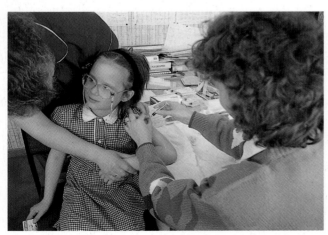

▲ Today, children can be vaccinated against illnesses such as measles and whooping cough.

Jenner experimented by putting some cowpox into the arm of a local boy. The boy got cowpox, but soon recovered. Then Jenner deliberately infected him with smallpox. The boy did not get smallpox – the cowpox had made him immune. This was the first **vaccine**.

Since Jenner's day vaccines have been developed for many other diseases such as polio, which was a killer into the 20th century.

Louis Pasteur links germs with disease

Louis Pasteur (1822 – 95), a French scientist, was studying wine to see why it went bad. He looked at the wine through a **microscope** and saw millions of **bacteria** living in it. When he heated the wine, he discovered that the bacteria were killed. *See p.17* ◀

He also found that the wine stayed in good condition if it was in a sealed container, but as soon as it was exposed to the air, the bacteria reappeared and it went bad again.

◀ Bacteria need air and a medium temperature to grow.

From these experiments, Pasteur reasoned that bacteria from the air were getting into the wine and causing it to decay. Further experiments showed him that some airborne bacteria also caused disease.

His discoveries led him to introduce the **pasteurization** of milk and beer by heating them to kill off bacteria.

▲ Louis Pasteur in his laboratory, using a microscope to look at bacteria

Hospital pioneers

▲ An operation taking place with an antiseptic carbolic spray being used to kill bacteria.

At the beginning of the 19th century hospitals were dirty places and many patients died from infections. Methods of surgery were still quite primitive and most operations were to **amputate** limbs. If patients did not bleed to death during these operations, they were likely to die of shock from having the operation without anything to kill the pain.

The introduction of pain-killing **anaesthetics** was a great step forward in surgery. One early anaesthetic, ether, was first introduced in America in 1846. Another type, chloroform, was first demonstrated in 1847 by a Scottish doctor, Sir James Simpson.

Joseph Lister introduces antiseptic

Even after the introduction of anaesthetics many patients died after operations. Often this was because their wounds became infected. An English surgeon, Joseph Lister (1827 – 1912) read Louis Pasteur's work on **bacteria** and realized that germs on people and medical instruments could infect his patients.
See Pasteur p.19 ◀

He introduced an **antiseptic**, called carbolic acid, to kill germs. At first, this was used to soak the bandages. Later it was used as a spray.

Florence Nightingale

Florence Nightingale (1820–1910), an English nurse, devoted her life to nursing and became the founder of nursing as a proper profession. In 1854 she took a team of nurses to the town of Scutari during the Crimean War and was horrified to find soldiers dying in filthy conditions.

She worked tirelessly to improve the standard of nursing at the hospital, and after a few months, there was a fall in the number of soldiers who died from their wounds.

Florence Nightingale later founded a school for nurses where they could be properly trained. She also helped to set up the Red Cross organization.

▼ Florence Nightingale (above) became known among her hospital patients as "the Lady of the Lamp".

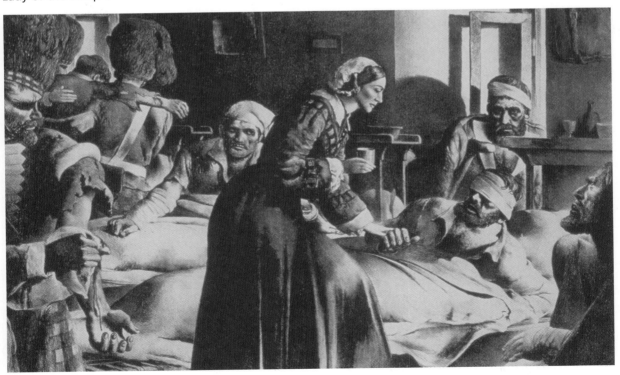

Marie Curie
explores radioactivity

A big step forward in medicine came at the end of the 19th century with the discovery of **X-rays**. This allowed doctors to look into the body without cutting it open. The most important work on X-rays was carried out by a Polish scientist, Marie Curie (1867–1934) and her husband Pierre.

X-rays, which were discovered in 1895 by a German scientist, Wilhelm Röntgen, are rays which can pass through most of the body but are absorbed by the bones and other hard parts of the insides, such as **tumours** and **gallstones**.

▼ Early X-ray machines were called fluoroscopes. A bellows camera was placed over the part of the body to be X-rayed. The bones block out the rays, leaving shadows of their shape

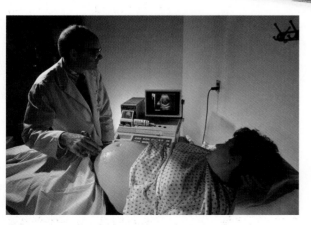

▲ Repeated doses of X-rays can be harmful. Today, we have a new method of looking inside the body, using **ultrasonic scanners**. They can look into a pregnant woman's womb to build up a picture of the unborn child.

Three years after Röntgen's discovery, the Curies took his discovery a step further. In 1898 they discovered radium, which they extracted from an ore called pitchblende. They found that radium emitted powerful rays that could heal wounds. Further work showed that these rays could cure diseased cells and destroy some **cancers**.

Alexander Fleming
and penicillin

▼ Penicillin saved the lives of many wounded soldiers during the Second World War.

Another major discovery at the beginning of the 20th century was something many of us take for granted today – **antibiotics**. In 1928 a Scottish researcher, Alexander Fleming (1881–1955) discovered that a certain sort of **mould**, called *Penicillium*, could be used to kill deadly germs.

The development of Fleming's discovery was the work of another doctor, the Australian Howard Florey (1898–1968) and his team. Florey tested the penicillin drug on mice and it was first given to a patient in 1940. The patient improved whilst taking the penicillin, but died once supplies of the drug ran out. This proved that penicillin worked.

This stained-glass window, showing Alexander Fleming in his laboratory, is in a church in Paddington, London, close to St Mary's Hospital where he worked. ▶

Once people knew about penicillin there was a big demand for it. However, there was not enough to go round. During the Second World War the American government gave money so that penicillin could be produced on a massive scale.

DNA and the double helix

For thousands of years no one knew why people looked the way they did and why they inherited certain **characteristics** from their parents. In 1865, a monk called Gregor Mendel discovered a pattern in the way characteristics are handed down from parent to child, generation after generation.

▲ Characteristics such as the colour of the eyes and hair are passed from parents to children through their genes.

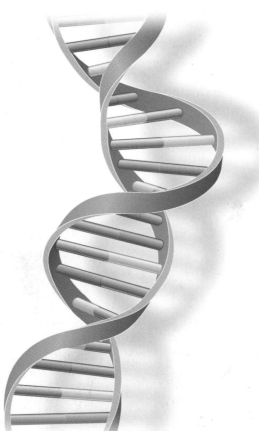

▲ DNA has two intertwined strands. This shape is known as a double helix. The cross bars between the strands contain genetic information.

Nearly a century later, scientists discovered a substance called DNA (**d**eoxyribo**n**ucleic **a**cid) which is stored in all living things. DNA is found in **genes**, which are tiny parts of cells that affect what living things look like and the way in which they develop. People inherit characteristics from their parents because genetic information is stored and passed on by the DNA in the cells.

Crick and Watson

The structure of the DNA molecule was officially discovered in 1953 by Francis Crick and James Watson, but much of the research which led to the final results was carried out by Rosalind Franklin (1920–57).

Franklin and Wilkins

Rosalind Franklin began her scientific work in Paris and in 1950 she began to study DNA at King's College, London. She discussed her work with other scientists and gave lectures on it, little realizing that Crick and Watson, who were studying DNA at Cambridge, England, were racing against her, trying to be first to reach the answer.

Crick and Watson won the race and were first to publish their findings, in 1953. But Rosalind Franklin and her fellow scientist Maurice Wilkins had made an enormous contribution to their work.

▲ Rosalind Franklin died before her important work on DNA became widely known. However, Watson, Crick, and Wilkins were jointly awarded the Nobel Prize in 1962.

The work on DNA enabled scientists to identify genetic diseases (those which are passed down through a family) and led to genetic engineering, in which scientists try to find ways of treating and preventing these diseases.

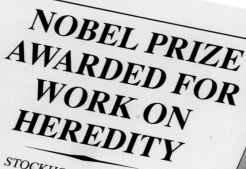

NOBEL PRIZE AWARDED FOR WORK ON HEREDITY

Dr James Watson

Dr Francis Crick

STOCKHOLM October 18

Two Britons and an American were today jointly awarded this year's Nobel Prize for medicine for work on heredity. The Britons are Dr. Francis ...ck and Dr. Maurice Wilkins. The American, ...James Watson, is Professor of Biology at ...rd, and worked at Cambridge, England in ...2.

...ssor Ulf von Euler, Chairman of the ... Institute's Nobel committee, which ...medicine prize winners, said the work ...'s winners was of great importance to

the whole study of hereditary diseases.

CODE DISCOVERED

The work of the trio, meant, in effect, the discovery of a code, or working instructions, for the formation of enzymes which govern heredity. This was another link in the work of making clear the whole blueprint for the production of living beings, he said. It could lead to an expla... why one species was dif...

...CE CAN BE F...
...XFORD...

25

Modern surgery

In the last hundred years, **surgical** skills and equipment have become very advanced. Very effective **anaesthetics** and **antiseptics** are widely used and spare blood can be stored until it is needed.

Apart from the basic surgical instruments, such as scalpels for cutting into the body and forceps for gripping or pulling, surgeons now use a range of more complex instruments and machines. They try to do as little damage as possible by using machines such as X-rays and **scanners** to see inside the body without cutting it. When they do cut the body, they often use "keyhole" surgery, working through tiny cuts. The old-style scalpel can be replaced with a **laser** scalpel that has a very precise beam for cutting.

An endoscope is an instrument for looking into parts of the body, using laser beams. It is flexible, so it can "see round corners".

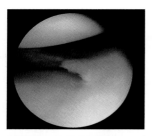

◀ A torn knee cartilage as seen through an endoscope

▼ An arthroscope is a type of endoscope for looking inside joints, such as the knees.

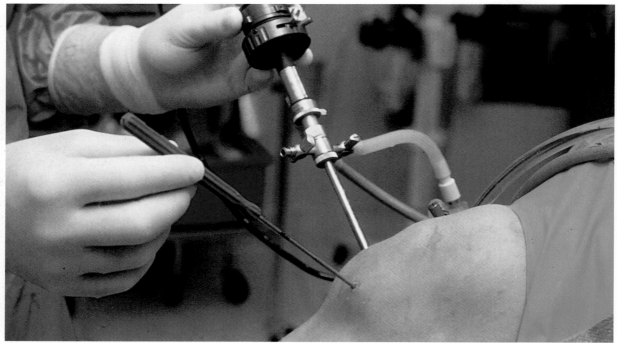

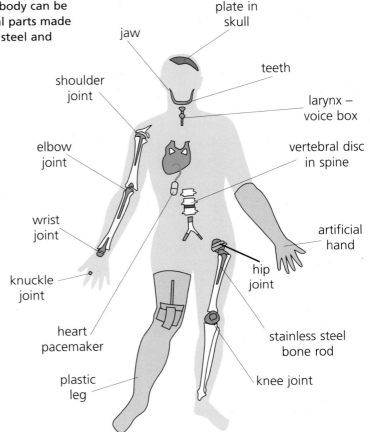

▶ Many parts of the body can be replaced with artificial parts made from plastic, stainless steel and other materials.

plate in skull

jaw

teeth

shoulder joint

larynx – voice box

elbow joint

vertebral disc in spine

wrist joint

artificial hand

knuckle joint

hip joint

heart pacemaker

stainless steel bone rod

plastic leg

knee joint

New for old

Today, people can be fitted with new "spare parts" to replace joints or **organs** which do not work properly. Putting an artificial part, such as a hip joint, into a patient is called an **implant**. Putting in a living organ, such as a kidney, is called a **transplant**.

John Charnley

Artificial joints offer pain relief for people with **arthritis** and similar bone problems. The first successful hip operation was carried out by an English surgeon, John Charnley, in 1960. Today, hundreds of hip replacements are carried out each day throughout the world.

Christiaan Barnard

South African surgeon Christiaan Barnard performed the first heart transplant in 1967. The patient only lived for 18 days, but today many patients receiving new organs survive for many years. The successful transplant of other organs, such as livers, lungs, and kidneys followed during the 1970s.

DEAD GIRL'S HEART TRANSPLANTED

Sick man given new hope after unique operation

Mr. Louis Washkansky, a 56 year old businessman, was making satisfactory progress in Groote Schuur hospital, Cape Town, today, 12 hours after receiving the transplant of a complete heart. The donor was a 25 year old woman, Miss Denise Ann Darvall, who was mortally injured when she and her mother were knocked down by a car. Her mother was killed

Professor Christiaan Barnard

▲ Barnard became world-famous after his first successful heart transplant.

What next?

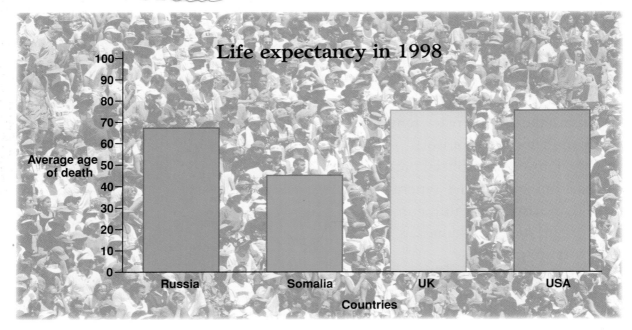

Life expectancy in 1998

Average age of death

100
90
80
70
60
50
40
30
20
10
0

Russia   Somalia   UK   USA

Countries

Medicine today has come a long way since the early attempts at primitive brain **surgery**, magic spells, and curious "potions". All the men and women in this book were lifesavers, improving and extending our lives in a way that would have been thought "miraculous" in earlier ages. *See p.6–7* ←

Many of the major killer diseases have been wiped out and, in many countries, people who fall ill or have injuries can expect professional medical care and treatment from highly-trained doctors and nurses.

However, new diseases and illnesses still emerge and we rely on doctors and scientists to carry out research into what causes these diseases and to develop medicines that can cure them.

▲ How long can people in each country expect to live? **Life expectancy** varies, depending on the living conditions. Poverty can lead to an earlier death, but being wealthy does not always mean being healthy.

▲ One of the WHO's most successful campaigns was **immunization** against smallpox. By 1980 smallpox had been largely wiped out throughout the world.

Saving your own life

In the West, which is relatively rich, some people suffer from diseases linked to their lifestyle. For example, heart attacks can be triggered by eating too much of the wrong sorts of food, being overweight, and not taking enough exercise.

Epidemiology is the study of how and why diseases occur. Epidemiologists are now looking at the links between illness and diet, smoking, drinking alcohol, lack of sleep, and lack of exercise. This greater awareness of how these things affect our bodies means

▲ Fresh air and exercise keep people healthy.

that we can have greater control over our health. We can try to prevent some diseases before they even happen by making sure we live healthy, active lives.

▲ A healthy, balanced diet should include a variety of foods that provide protein, carbohydrate, fats, vitamins and minerals.

Rich and poor

Although highly successful medicines and treatments have been developed, they are not available to everyone. In developing countries, millions of people struggle to maintain their health despite poor **nutrition**, dirty water and lack of money for medicines and **vaccines**.

The World Health Organization (WHO) works with governments to try to improve medical conditions in different parts of the world.

Life and death

Although there are few official records, the average **life expectancy** in Europe in the early 14th century was about 30 years. Now it is 75 years.

Glossary

acupuncture The ancient Chinese medical technique of putting needles into certain points in the body to cure illnesses.

ailment Pain or illness.

amputate To cut off an arm or leg.

anaesthetic A drug for putting a patient to sleep during an operation.

anatomy The structure of the body.

antibiotic A drug which fights infections in the body.

antiseptic A purifying liquid which kills germs.

archaeologist A person who finds out about history by studying objects from the past.

arthritis Pains in the joints.

arthroscope An instrument for looking inside joints in the body.

bacteria A group of very tiny organisms, some of which cause disease.

cancer A harmful lump or growth in the body.

characteristics Qualities a person has, such as being musical or athletic.

chloroform A liquid used as an anaesthetic.

contagious Passed from person to person by personal contact.

devastating Destructive or overwhelming.

diagnosis A study of the facts about a person's illness to decide what it is.

dissecting Cutting the body into parts to study how it works.

endoscope An instrument for looking inside the body.

epidemic When a lot of people catch the same disease at nearly the same time.

epidemiology The study of how and why diseases occur.

ether A colourless liquid used as an anaesthetic.

gallstones Small stones in the gall bladder.

genes Tiny parts in each cell which affect what living things look like and how they develop.

graft To fix a new piece (usually of skin) on to a person so that it becomes part of that person.

hygiene Keeping things clean and healthy.

immune Protected against a disease.

implant To put an artificial part into a patient.

inhale To breathe in.

laser A very narrow, powerful beam of light.

leech A small blood-sucking animal related to the earthworm.

life expectancy The number of years a person can expect to live.

microscope An instrument for studying things that are too tiny to be seen with the naked eye.

molecule A very small part of any substance.

mould A type of fungus.

nutrition Food for growth.

organ An important body part.

pasteurization A method of killing germs by intense heat treatment.

patient Person having treatment from a doctor.

pilgrimage A journey to a place of worship.

radioactive Sending out powerful rays which can penetrate solid materials.

radium A radioactive element used to treat certain diseases such as cancer.

scanner A machine for looking inside the body.

sterilize To destroy germs by treatment such as great heat.

surgery Cutting into the body to carry out an operation.

symptoms Particular signs of a disease.

theory Idea or explanation.

tourniquet A tight band fixed round a limb to slow down blood flow.

transplant To replace a damaged organ, such as the heart, with a healthy living organ from someone else.

trepanning Drilling holes in the head to let out evil spirits in Stone Age times.

tumour Unhealthy lump growing in the body.

ultrasonic Beyond the range of human hearing.

urine Liquid waste that passes out of the body.

vaccine A substance which makes the body resistant to a disease.

vapours Gases or fumes.

virus The smallest known type of living thing which causes disease.

X-rays Rays which can penetrate soft substances but are stopped by hard ones.

Books for further reading

Medicine through Time by Fiona Reynolds, Foundations of History series, published by Heinemann

Timelines – Medicine by Kathryn Senior, published by Franklin Watts

Medicine by Pam Beesant, Usborne Young Scientist, published by Usborne

Medicine and Health by Nigel Hawkes, "New Technology" series, published by Gloucester Press

The History News – Medicine by Phil Gates, published by Walker Books

Index

acupuncture   6
amputation   4, 15, 20
anaesthetics   20, 26
arthroscope   26
artificial joints   27
artificial limbs   15, 27
Avicenna   8

bacteria   17, 19
Barnard, Christiaan   27
blood circulation   5, 9, 16
blood–letting   11

CAT scanner   5
Charnley, John   27
Chinese medicine   6
Cosmos and Damian   10
Crick, Francis   24–5
Curie, Marie   5, 22

da Vinci, Leonardo   14
diagnosis   8, 10
diet   29
DNA   24–5
dissection   15

Egyptian medicine   7
endoscope   26
epidemiology   29

Fleming, Alexander   23
Florey, Howard   23
Franklin, Rosalind   24–5

Galen   9

Harvey, William   16
herbal medicine   4, 6, 10
Hippocrates   8
Hipppocratic Oath   8
hospitals   10, 20–21
Hunter, William and John   17

Imhotep   7
implants   27
Indian nose grafts   7

Islamic medicine   8
Jenner, Edward   18

laser scalpel   26
leeches   5, 16
leprosy   13
life expectancy   28
Lister, Joseph   20

medical schools   11, 15
medieval medicine   10

Mendel, Gregor   24
microscope   17, 19

Nightingale, Florence   5, 21
nose grafts   7

organ transplants   5, 27

Paracelsus   14
Paré, Ambroise   15
Pasteur, Louis   19, 20
penicillin   23
Plague   4, 12–13

Rhases   8
Röntgen, Wilhelm   22

Simpson,   Sir James 20
smallpox   5, 18
surgery   15, 17, 26–7

trepanning   6

ultrasonic scanners   22, 26

vaccines   5, 18, 29
Vademecum   10
van Leeuwenhoek, Anthony   17
Vesalius, Andrea   5, 15
viruses   4

Watson, James   24–5
Wilkins, Maurice   25
wise women   10
World Health Organization   28–9

X-rays   22, 26